(Prologue)

(Prologue)

JEANIE TOMASKO

Concrete Wolf
Poetry Chapbook Series

ISBN 978-0-9797137-9-8

Design by Tonya Namura
using Minion Pro

Cover and inside Art: Judith Bellinghausen Mayer
Author photo: Steve Tomasko

2013 Editor's Choice Award Winner
made possible by a generous grant from M

Concrete Wolf Poetry Chapbook Series

Concrete Wolf
PO Box 1808
Kingston, WA 98346

http://ConcreteWolf.com

ConcreteWolf@yahoo.com

For Bärbel, wherever she may be.

(The Province of Grammar: A Partial Map)

gram *or* **gramme** \'gram\ *n* [F gramme, fr. LL *gramma*, a small weight, fr. Gk *grammat-*, *gramma* letter, writing, a small weight, fr. *graphein* to write—more at CARVE] (1797) :

-**gram** \'gram\ *n comb form* : drawing : writing : record <chrono*gram*> <tele*gram*>

grammar \'gram-ər\ *n* [ME *gramere*, fr. MF *gramaire*, Gk *grammatikē*, fr. fem. of *grammatikos* of letters, fr. *grammat-*, *gramma*—more at GRAM] **1 a** : the study of the classes of words, their inflections and their functions and relations[a] **2 a** : general truth on which all truths or stories can be based, as in *if you live by the coast, you learn the coast's grammar* **b** : rules of a language to be used when speaking and/or walking near an ocean
c : the writing down of the rules as in a grammar book or, on the sand **d** : the way things are said **e** : the way (some) things are (not) said e.g., **ungrammar** **f** : gramatica, Span, fem.
g : all of the sentences permissible on a given day as opposed to **grammarless** *adj* all of those not permissible on Tuesdays **h** : a secret language of the body; a ghost that needs to be told
i : a country e.g., the Province of Grammar **j** : *no one can tell a story without grammar*

gratitude \'grat-ə-t(y)üd*n* [L *gratus* grateful] **1** : THANKFULNESS **2** : for Steve and Cliff and Sandy who believed in Teej and lobsters from the beginning **3** : for Mary, who always "just knows," and **4** : for Steve, again, who understands everything

[a] everything preceding (a) from Webster's Ninth New Collegiate Dictionary, 1986 Merriam-Webster Inc., p. 531

…and for her, whose face I held in my hands a few hours, whom I gave back only to keep holding the space where she was, I light a small fire in the rain.

— Galway Kinell, The Book of Nightmares

Listen to the broccoli.

— Anne Lamott

If a whale has a proper name

It is a Tuesday afternoon, late May, and a good year for whales.
A thousand crows patrol the salt marsh.
Whales are large animals. Whales are mammals. Whale is a noun.

This isn't the problem. The problem is there are two nouns for almost everything in the world. Heart, for example. Heart is a noun. But take it out of the chest and it beats like *want* in someone else's hand. Or, summer. Summer is a noun, but also an illusion. On any other day, you recall a particular one, and what comes to you is a handful of blueberries. A walk in the woods is a noun. In the branches, the forest birds are singing the songs you remember, but backwards. They sing to name the hungers of the world. Hunger is a noun. The other word for hunger is heart. The heart is hungry for air. A lighthouse is air except for light and loneliness. A noun is the name of a person, place or thing.

1. Lighthouse was always a name for summer.
2. Sometimes it was Tuesday afternoon.
3. Love was a noun and a thing.
4. Tide, lighthouse, afternoon, sorrow, whale…
5. The look in a whale's eyes was a thing and there was a word for it.
6. A love story starts anywhere it wants to, even on a Tuesday in May. It's only proper.

it is called a Proper Noun

It is not all important to find a beginning because

In one beginning there were three nouns: air, breast, arms. These are the first nouns that need no nouns, the first words that can't be named. The first three wants. It's like that in this sort of beginning. In another beginning there was want and longing, but differently. In both beginnings there was a girl. She had an old faded memory of something happy. There was a lighthouse in the third beginning, but it was occupied, so she started at the second beginning. The first beginning begins before birth, in darkness; a darkness that is warm and safe and never questioned. But then there is light, which forever is. The girl had been born in the morning at low tide in the Summer of the Whale. She was made out of what came before and what came before that. She returned to the sea, five Summers of the Whale later. You know the story. The other word for story is sea.

so far there are four beginnings

Tell me how it starts then

We were what they call in Maine, *summer people*, or *from away*. *From away* is another word for Canada, or Nebraska. She was from Canada and we were both eleven. Her real name was Petra.[1] A magnet has a north pole and a south. It knows the word, *inseparable*, without saying it. We were eleven and she was homesick. I gave her a shell and she put it up to her ear while our fathers picked out lobsters from the large saltwater tank behind the restaurant. We thought lobsters were inseparable from the sea but we were wrong. We were right that spiders defy gravity. They can stay in the same place on a ceiling for weeks. You think gravity would pull them down seeing how it is supposed to keep your feet on the ground. It was a Tuesday, and the only thing that stayed in place was the moon. I called her Pete and she called me Teej.

---

[1] Petra is a name, a noun. It means summer and rock. The world is made of rock. Rockpaperscissors. A summer is made of paper. The scissors come in later.

“Teej,”

“yeah,”

Have you checked the tide chart for today?

yeah.

I had a hard time saying the “r” in Petra the way she said it but she liked the name Pete. School had been out for two weeks already. My family arrived first and I started counting. I counted every day, maybe every hour of those two weeks and then suddenly, we had forever until August and nothing needed to be counted anymore. The other word for count is time. And when you are eleven or thirteen, the other word for time is endless. You barely notice that it slips by, and how fast. Summer is a word that doesn’t like to count. My real name is Tamlyn. Most everyone calls me TJ.

The sea wind blew from the southeast. We clambered down the old stone wall and landed on the big safe rock near a stretch of sand. A large turtle was sleeping there. The tide was going out, it was fairly calm. The sea air was that low tide mixture of salt and clam and kelp. We lay down and watched the turtle and Pete whispered, “last night my dad said if you count back seven generations, you’ll be related to someone famous.”

“Who are you related to?”

“Some pirate or something,” she said as the wind blew her long thin hair across her forehead, “but, I think I’m related to a spider or a turtle or a lobster.” She laughed. I laughed. We couldn’t stop. She said no one laughed that much in Canada.

“Is a spider a he, she or it?” one of us said.

She is an ambiguous pronoun;

Sometimes I is too. I can be telling the story, but I might not be the author. The book can be written by me or I or the author named on the front of this book. Other characters may include he, they, it, them, or Mr. or Mrs. So & So. In other words, when you don't want to say someone's name or disclose what they did, you can use a pronoun to refer to that which they had or might not have done. Without saying who is the storyteller. I am a storyteller. In the sentence: *she asked me to braid her hair*, she could mean a friend or a little sister. The me might be me, or not. Sometimes she is a pronoun used for the world or the moon or the sea. Consider, it. It was terrifying and beautiful at the same time. It could mean the ocean, or the braiding of her/my hair. Or the moon. Or, just it. *I wonder if you think about it* can mean many things. You are a reader of stories. You know that of which I speak could be anyone or anything. What *she* means is that pronouns can fool you.

Sometimes she refers to a sailing vessel

one steep grainy dark good first favorable whole most blueberry brick bricken plastic holy[b]

1. No one knows why a spider chooses a painted window ledge over a lighted sign, a morning prairie over a dark coastal forest, a cold apple storage basement over a corner bar. Could be hunger or fear. Could be time or luck. Could be it's as good a place as any. The first thread is the most difficult. But then, a favorable wind comes along and the spider's spanning thread takes hold on a pleasant morning under a blue sky.

2. No one knows why a spider chooses a _____ ledge over a _____ sign, a _____ prairie over a ________________ forest, a basement over a bar. The _____ thread is the most difficult. But then, a _____ wind comes along and the spider's _________ thread takes hold on a morning under a sky.

3. No one knows why a spider chooses a pleasant window ledge over a coastal sign, a lighted prairie over a first forest, a blue basement over a favorable bar. The apple storage thread is the most difficult. But then, a dark wind comes along and the spider's spanning thread takes hold on a morning morning under a cold and holy sky.

---

[b] adjective \'aj-ik-tiv\ … **2** : not standing by itself

rose clapboard small forgotten sienna damn rainy same summer glass Maine salty apple cold

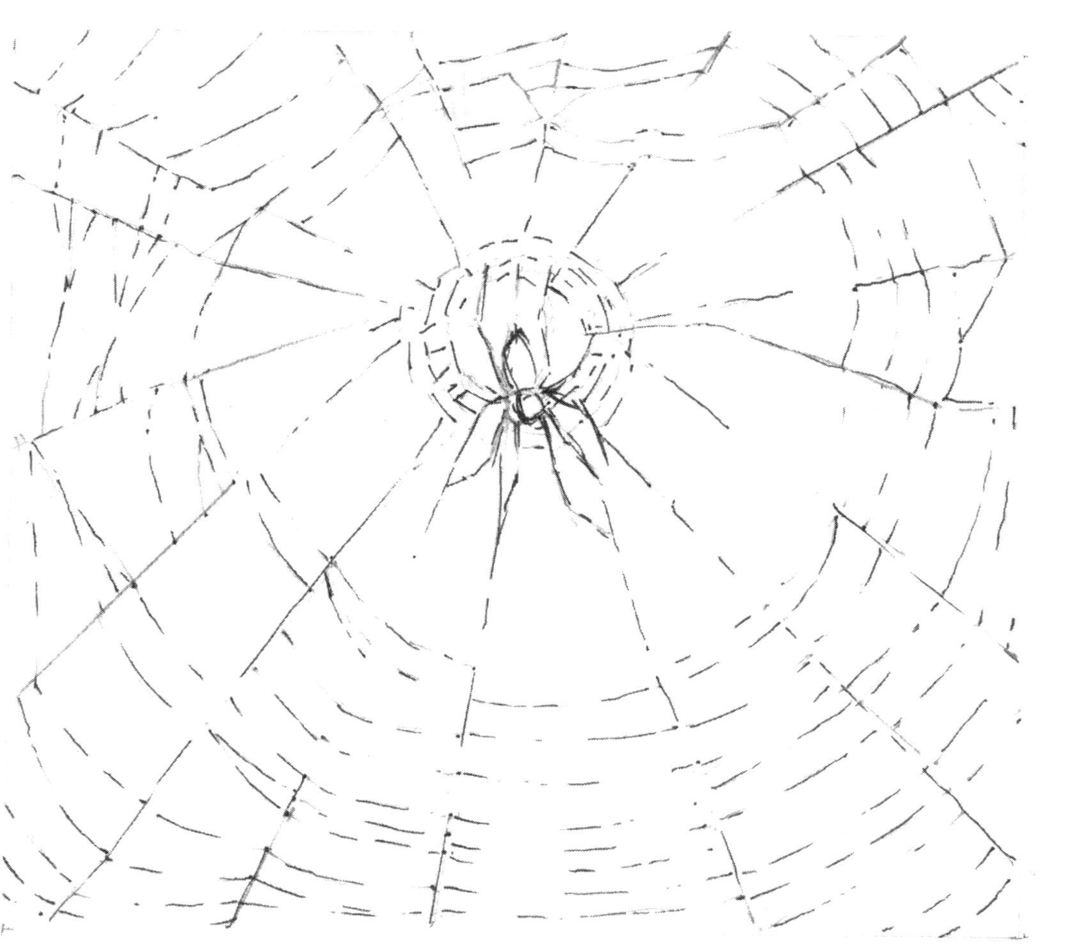

An adjective primer with a spider in it and

No one knows how the (blue hammock-shaped) moon got there.
No one knows why a (brown yellow) spider chooses a (painted window) ledge over a (lighted hardware) sign.
No one knows why a (morning) prairie or a (dark coastal) forest, a (cold apple storage) basement or a (corner Portland) bar.
No one knows what comes before the spider, why (two) girls, what it is about Tuesdays.
No one knows the (   ) story.
They say the (spider's first) thread is the most difficult. But if there is (some) luck, a (favorable) wind comes along and the (spanning) silk takes hold on a (pleasant ocean) morning under a (blue) sky.
No one knows the (length) strength of silk.
No one knows why there was (once) a (summer) morning under

a (cold and holy) sky

Space for your own story and what the narrator remembered:

[

]

[I wake up mornings with one arm stretched out above my head and one on my blueberry chest. I know I've always slept that way because someone took a photograph of me in the holy house with the steep and methodist stairs. I don't know how my arms end up where they do, though it might have something to do with spiders. The grainy photograph on my desk knows the story. That old window I slept under probably knows too, but won't give away its glass secrets. It was cold there under the forgotten window, I remember that much. Small rose-colored spiders would stay in the same place for weeks at a time. When it was warm, I'd watch them spin. I remember thinking that somewhere in a Maine spider is a bricken stillness. I know now that somewhere in my body there's a place like that too, a pool of brackish water that remembers things the rest of me has forgotten. Stories that can translate the difficult world of the body. Stories that can tell me who I am. Stories that can get me to the coastal apple rain of the deal. That can unspin the messy web and get me to the very first thread, the place the body inside knows by heart. Stories tell the whole bloody truth. It feels like a wound. The other word for wound is grace.]

"What did you say about spiders, Pete?"

"Lobsters, Teej."

Tell me a story then, about a lobster

"Mmmmm, let's see. Once upon a time there was a girl who lived on an island made of diamonds. It was an apple island that sparkled in the sun and on nights when the moon was full it would glow an Episcopalian blue. She wanted to go somewhere else though, like most girls do. But, there was no way to leave the island. And it was foretold that she would be a coastal nun. One day she was working in the church garden and a grainy man came to the gate. He was dressed all in red. His eyes were kind of like a lobster's beadglasseyes. She had never seen him before on the island. She gathered some carrots and potatoes in a basket woven from seaweed and took it over to where he was, because the nuns were known for giving their vegetables to all who passed by. She handed him the basket and when she saw his eyes up close, she saw a catholic (with a small c) ocean with high waves pounding a bricken shore. He said, 'In return for the basket, I will give you three words.' 'What should I do with the words?' she asked, mesmerized by the waves. 'At the next full moon, you must pick one word and say it when the night bells ring at 3.' So, seven days later, when the moon was full and the apple island was glowing blue, the girl said "lobster" at 3 in the morning."

"Did the lobster bite?" I asked.

"No." she said.

Did the man have a scar?

How did you know?

review *v* **1** : to look back **2** : to unforget **3** : to look into, as

A noun is the name of a person, place or whale.
The first nouns you remembered from the Fifth Summer were air and lighthouse.
The lighthouse was taken.
There are two words for every word.
Both, is another word for two, e.g., a word and its adjective.
Body is another other word for memory.
Memory is a (rearview) mirror.
Mirrors look back and are/are not reliable.
I never remember what I look like.
Even with a picture of a lobster in your hand.
In the picture you have a (whale-shaped) scar.
A scar is what happened and what didn't.
A spider wove by a cold painted window.
The first thread was/is the most bricken.

in a rearview mirror

the form/forms of the verb *is*

am is are were was

We *were* eleven.
She *was* homesick.
We *are* in Maine.
We *were* in Maine.
I *was* eleven too.

Is *is* as big as being.
Love *is* a noun in a story on a Tuesday.
Is *is* a verb.

should be would be want to be would I be

His/her whole frame *was* trembling.
Is, present singular
Was, past singular
Were, past plural, as in she and I were
Are, present(ly)

must might shall will may can

Am. Me. Now. I am. I must may might be am in love.

are very irregular

Is that how

you got to Maine," I asked, "I mean by saying, *lobster*?"

"There was a spider in the story, too."

"What?"

"Teej, there was a spider in the corner of the girl's dressing room a long time before she was a nun and it was a talking spider that only she could hear. One time the spider said a secret thing."

"What?"

"If someone ever gives you three words, you must take them."

I had an old hairbrush in my satchel and I took it out and began to brush her brown, longer-than-summer hair.

"Why?"

Because a spider starts out with three threads and it's the way things work. The tide was still ebbing.

What three words are you thinking of? she asked.

Mmmmm. Whale, mermaid, octopus.[2]

---

[2] The names, or nouns, of the first three wants. The first nouns you know without nouns. The names you name without knowing.

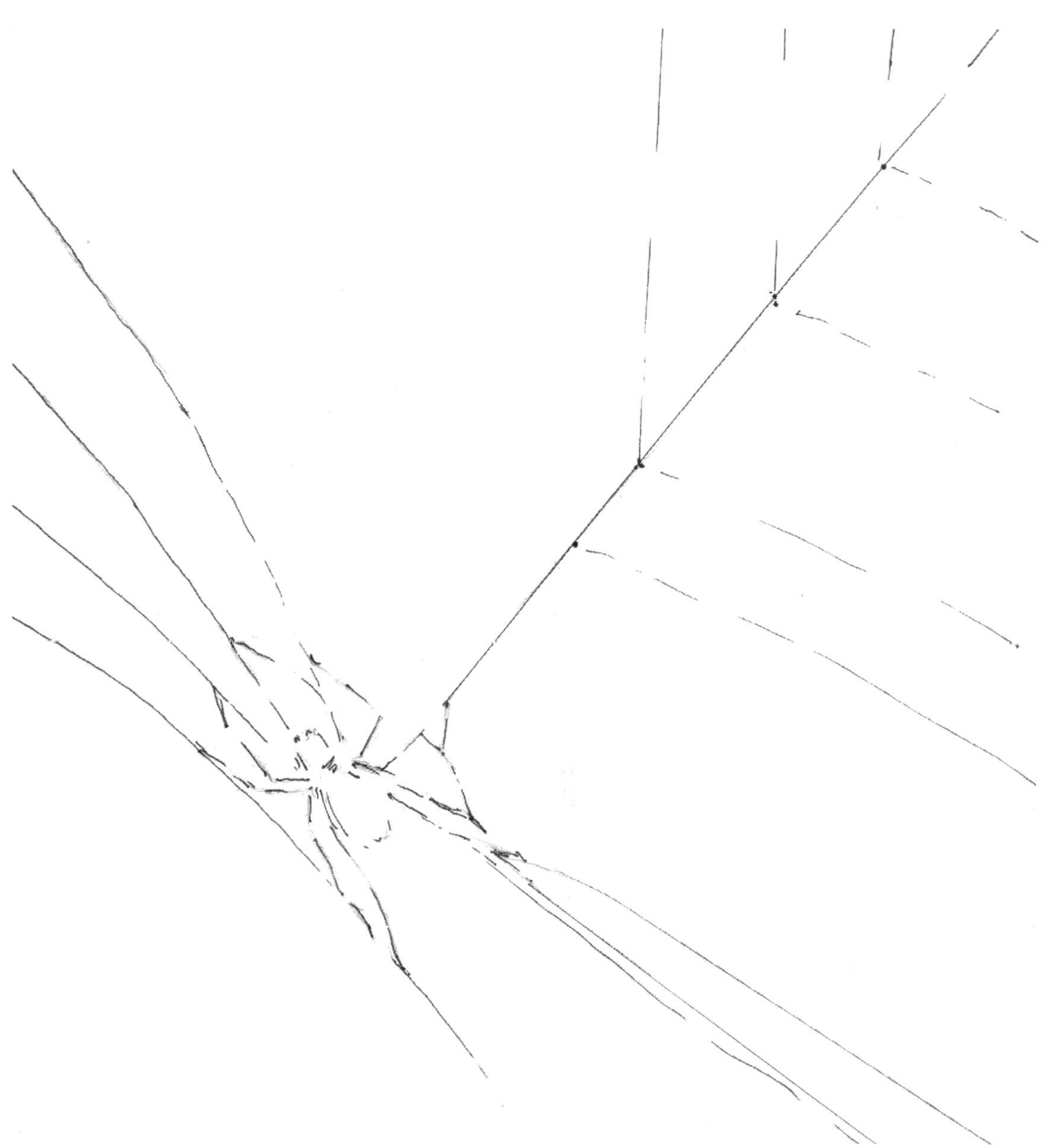

22. How a spider spins

The first thread that the spider throws, after the wind and the luck, is called the spanning thread. If it takes hold and is secure, the spider runs silk back and forth to form a cable. When the cable is thick enough, it is called the bridge thread. Then she drops a loose line that hangs like a half-circle, or the part of the moon that shows below a cloud. She climbs down the bottom of the cloud and pulls the loose thread tight with another thread and secures it. And that's the beginning of the web. She adds frame threads to secure the edges, radius threads for walking on and eating and a signal line for communications. The moon doesn't stay in place.

using a cloud, the moon, some wind (and verbs[c])

[c] **verb** \'vərb\ *n* [ME *verbe*, fr. MF, fr. L *verbum*] : a word that characteristically is the grammatical center of a predicate and expresses an act, occurrence or mode of being, that in various languages is inflected … for tense, for voice, for mood, or for aspect …

ver-bal-ism \'vər-bə-liz-əm\ *n* … **2** : words used as if they were more important than the realities they represent

ver-ba-tim \ vər-'bāt-əm\ *adj* : in the exact words : WORD FOR WORD, WHALE FOR WHALE

ver-bo-ten \vər-'bōt-n\ *adj* : to forbid : not allowed : FORBIDDEN :

verge \'vərj\ *n* : **3** : something that borders, limits or bounds **4** : outer margin **5** : the edge **6** : to incline toward the horizon, to be on the verge or border

I divided her hair into three sections,

Hold the whale with your left hand.

Hold the octopus with your right.

Let the mermaid fall down the middle of the back.

Cross the whale over the mermaid and grab the whale with the octopus.

Now grab the mermaid with your whale and let the whale fall down the middle.

Cross the octopus over the whale and grab the octopus with the mermaid.

The octopus was strange and beautiful and the whale loved her exceedingly but he didn't have arms and he didn't know any of the words for love. Love is a story. *Once I loved*, is a verb.

a whale, a mermaid and an octopus

23. Some facts about sentences.

Birds fly.

A sentence is made of language.

Language is made of signs.

Bird is the sign. *Birds fly* is all you need.

The Summer of the Whale needs a verb, or a bird.

Sheer language can convince.

A story is a series of birds that may or may not fly.

If you love ghosts, write a ghost sentence.

If you love *love*, write a love sentence.

Bookstores have maps of The Province of Grammar.

Make sure the reader can get to the ocean.

Exercise: Using eight parts of speech, in under 100 words, name your ghost and color it in.

[Summer is a noun. She and I are pronouns. Low is an adjective for tide. "We could go" is a complete verb phrase. "Against all odds" is a fragment with a preposition in it. The adverb is carefully. "With a little luck and a little wind" is a wish that the thread will catch. The spider says to herself, *yes!* [*inter*]]

Tell me more then, against all odds, before time

"When does the mermaid come in?" I asked.

"After the prepositions."

"What!?"

(Once upon)

The octopus lived at the bottom of the sea. She had eight arms. She had three hearts. With one of her hearts she loved a whale. With one of her hearts she loved darkness at the bottom of the sea. With one of her hearts she kept a secret. The secret was to be busy with all of her arms like a person who keeps checking to see if their jello is set yet, while writing a book while walking while getting the mail. This is so she doesn't have time to think about love or whales. The whale didn't care about jello or refrigerators or mailboxes. She swam and longed for two things. One was an arm to wrap around something. She didn't know her eyes were so beautiful and sad and could do all the wrapping that an arm could. The other was to say one word that would make all the difference.

"What did the whale want to say?" I asked.

"The whale and the octopus wanted to love each other but they couldn't," she said.

beside the sea, beneath what you see, within the whale, against all, beyond

Fill in the blanks

The edge[3] _____ the sea is hard to define.

The space _____ waves is a silence few enter.

We never know what we are up against.

She was _____ the north of somewhere.

I could have sat _____ her for the rest of my life.

(abovebelowaroundinbybesidealongfromagainstbetweenbeneathoverintonexttoalongsideof foreverforever)

with prepositions

[3] edge

You can stand on the edge of something and call it secret and lovely. You can fall off, or not. You can jump off and be lost forever. The edge of the sea keeps changing. If the tide is out, the edge is out. If the edge is out, you can walk along and look for tide pools. The other word for edge is hard to come by. An edge needs a preposition. A frame thread is an edge. The days of summer are frame threads. Frame threads are like buoys that hold and keep. We had no idea what we were doing. We were just kids playing the edge.

24. Poetry: with/without paying attention

"Let's write a poem about that."

"Ok, I'll start."

The octopus was beautiful and the whale loved her exceedingly but

He didn't know how to eat dreams. When I eat dreams I take a spoon

And a fork so if the night gets really dark and I can't see the whales

You will travel with a whale and an orange suitcase, the fortune said, *unless*

You travel inside the whale (and that's a fairy tale). In the fairy tale, once

Upon a time, the girl walked along the beach and she knew she had

The fortune. A fisherman told her how to swallow the low tide, how to

Know the whale by heart, how to throw a rope and dream about whales.

She went to the sea every morning after that to learn the tides

By chart. A man in a cabin was painting a whale. What is her name

She asked. *Salt*. It is a beautiful name, (you said)

“It is a beautiful whale.”

“And there’s a mermaid in the picture, too, with a shiny tail.”

I don’t believe in them anymore, Teej.

You don’t?[4]

[4] ? A question is a part of speech. e.g., What are you painting? What is the whale’s name? Some questions are hard to answer, e.g., *can one memory carry you through a lifetime*?

The other word for looking-glass is

tidal pool

boundary

geology

silver

silver sea water

At low tide, the reef is scattered with tidal pools filled with urchins, anemones, snails, crabs and clams.

"Teej, come over here, it's like one of those Easter egg things you look into, all sparkly and stuff."

The floor was a soft green moss, the water clear as a mirror. There were small starfish on the ceiling and they were perfectly reflected in the watermirror.

We stayed as long as we could.

"I wish we could sleep in here." someone said.

whatever helps you see

“HOW [*adv*] DID YOU SPEND THE SUMMER?”

So you tell them, “I divided her hair into three sections; a whale, a mermaid and an octopus.”

How, or in what manner? they ask.

So you say, “I divided her hair SLOWLY into three large whales.” Where slowly is an *adverb of manner.*

Add an adverb, they say, *to “The whale swallowed the entire sea.”*

“The whale CAREFULLY swallowed the entire sea making sure he did not swallow the octopus he loved.”

And then they go on to say *adverbs of time* answer the question, “When?” as in: now, then, soon, forever ago,

tomorrow, tonight, Tuesday …

“Like this,” Pete said, “LAST NIGHT the whale swallowed the entire sea except the octopus.

CAREFULLY.”

“Where was the octopus?” I asked. *Adverbs of place* can answer this.

“She was over THERE, where those rocks stick out into the ocean. It’s not as FAR as it looks. Wanna walk over THERE this afternoon?"

"Sure."

"How did the octopus know the whale was swallowing the sea?" I asked.

"The same way a spider knows there is food in its web."

"How?" I asked.

,they write on the board every September

analysis Gk, **1** : act of breaking up e.g., sentences

9. Analysis | helps you get at the meaning of a thought.

14. Practice in analysis | ought to assist us | to be clear.

e.g., *The river | glideth | at his own sweet will.*

The last line the spider spins | is a signal thread | or vibration line.

The spider | can tell by the vibration if it's wind | fly | or its mate.

Low tides | come when summer | begins to vibrate.

Girls | can tell by vibration | when it's the end | of summer.

The vibration of summer | is not what you want.

If you live by the sea | keep | a tide chart handy.

A tide chart | is | only a prediction.

Disclaimer: | The sea | may act on its own.

"Oh!"[5]

The ocean | will always remind you of | _________.

For the fly | vibration means | The End.

---

[5] interjection (*interj*) e.g., *My! How you've grown!* and/or *Oh! You stopped believing in whales*?

And they remind you to use

To What Extent? i.e., exceedingly, barely, very, secretly, wholly, (holy), always, never

So you write your paper and you say to them, "Does this answer how[6] I spent my summer?"

---

[6] word by word, story by story, very happy, sitting by the sea, shoulders barely touching, braiding the octopus, swallowing the whale, secretly believing in mermaids, never counting

adverbs of degree

Memorization, or things to know

A noun is the name of a person, place or thing.

The vibration of summer is a place and a thing.

"Teej, what do you know by heart?"

"The octopus has three hearts." I said.

"What does she do if she uses one up?"

I don't know. A lobster can grow another arm.

But there is always a scar.

by heart

"WRITE FOUR ENDINGS[7] TO YOUR STORY WITH

and if but for if and for but and and if but and if if if only

~~and they lived happily ever after~~

~~but I never saw her again~~

~~if I could go back~~

For every life you choose there is one that goes on without you.[8]

/WITHOUT USING CONJUNCTIONS"

---

[7] the other word for ending is beginning

[8] see chap. 1

About the Artist

Judith Bellinghausen Mayer is an artist who grew up in Wisconsin and earned her BSA and MA from the University of Wisconsin, Madison. She divides her time between upstate New York and the Jersey Shore.

About the Author

Jeanie Tomasko is the author of *Tricks of Light* (Parallel Press), *Sharp as Want* (Little Eagle Press), a poetry / artworks collaboration with Sharon Auberle and the e-chapbook, *If I Confess Before 5:00* (Right Hand Pointing). Her work has been published in *The Midwest Quarterly, Right Hand Pointing, Rattle, Wisconsin People and Ideas* and *Birdsthumb*. She was the recipient of the Lorine Niedecker Poetry Award from The Council for Wisconsin Writers in 2014. The Collect of the Day is forthcoming from Centennial Press. She works as a home health nurse in Madison, WI.

17886325R00040

Made in the USA
Middletown, DE
13 February 2015